# The Careful Crocodile

Story by Beverley Randell

Illustrations by Ben Spiby

Long, long ago,
in the days of the dinosaurs,
a mother crocodile laid 40 eggs.
She laid the eggs
in a sandy nest by some ferns.

The sun kept the eggs warm.

Week after week, the mother crocodile
stayed under the ferns
to watch over her nest.

She did not go down to the lake
to eat and drink.
She had to take care of her eggs.

One day, a hungry dinosaur found the nest. The mother crocodile ran out of the ferns as fast as she could.

*Snap!* went her jaws.
And that was the end
of the egg-eating dinosaur!

The next day, some little cries came from the nest.

The mother crocodile went to the nest and pushed the sand away.
Yes! Baby crocodiles were coming out of the eggs.

Then the mother crocodile
opened her jaws
and filled them with baby crocodiles.

What **was** she doing?

The mother crocodile
was not **eating** her babies.
She was picking them up.
She wanted to take her babies
down to the lake
where they would find some food.

When the mother crocodile got to the lake,
she opened her jaws
and all the baby crocodiles swam out.

They saw some mayflies on the water.
**Snap!** went their little jaws.

13

Then the mother crocodile
hurried back to her nest.
She picked up the rest of her babies
and took **them**
down to the lake, too.

The baby crocodiles
grew bigger every day.
Sometimes they climbed
out of the water
to catch frogs and spiders
in the ferns.

And every day,
the mother crocodile
stayed near her babies and tried to keep them safe.